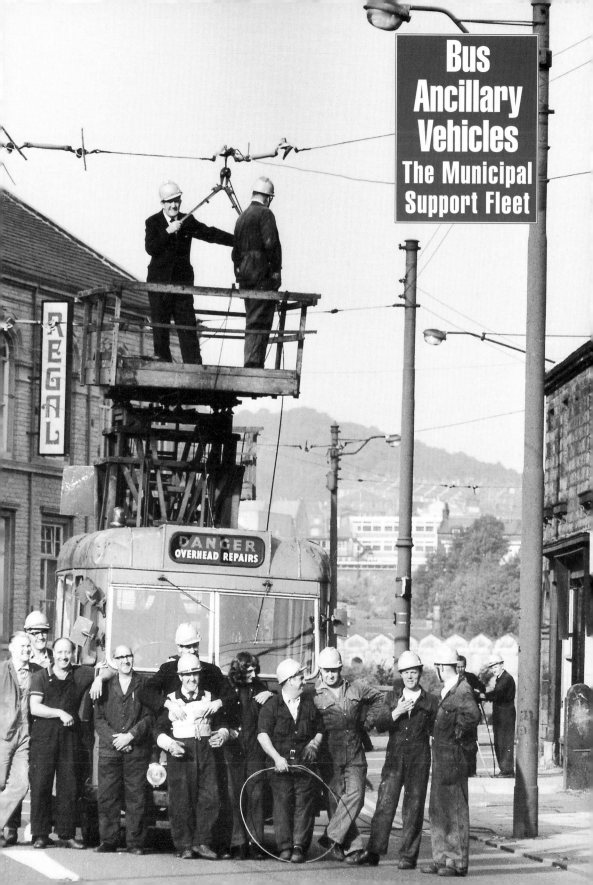

**Bus
Ancillary
Vehicles**
The Municipal
Support Fleet

Bus
Ancillary
Vehicles
The Municipal
Support Fleet

GAVIN BOOTH

Ian Allan PUBLISHING

Contents

Back cover colour photographs: upper:
This Dundee Corporation Daimler CVD6, new in 1951 with a Brush single-deck body, became a combined towing and tower wagon in 1968. *Arnold Richardson*

Back cover centre:
A considerably older vehicle is this solid-tyred Karrier tow wagon from the 1920s that survived intact for many years in Stockport Corporation's garage and is now preserved. *Photobus*

Back cover lower:
An Austin 16 car converted for use as a mobile canteen by Nottingham City Transport. *Ian Allan Library*

Half title page:
The overhead crew pose for a photograph as Herbert Emsley, Bradford Corporation's overhead foreman, prepares to cut the last length of trolleybus running wire on 13 August 1972. The Bradford trolleybus system closed in March 1972 — Britain's last — and this was the last length of wire to be cut in Britain. *B. A. Anderton*

Title page:
The PTEs did not stint when it came to recovery vehicles. This Foden was supplied to West Midlands PTE, here with a 1967 Daimler Fleetline/Park Royal on suspended tow. *Ian Allan Library*

First published 2001

ISBN 0 7110 2797 8

Published by Ian Allan Publishing

an imprint of Ian Allan Publishing Ltd, Hersham, Surrey KT12 4RG.
Printed by Ian Allan Printing Ltd, Hersham, Surrey KT12 4RG.

Code: 0109/B

Introduction

They were the forgotten vehicles in many municipal bus fleets. Those Cinderellas that we tended not to notice on the road or sitting in the back of depots and garages — wearing fleet livery often as not, and sometimes even with numbers. But did we pay sufficient attention to them? Probably not. Unless, of course, they were (or had been) buses, in which case we noted numbers, took photographs, acknowledged their existence.

Perhaps municipal fleets had more ancillary vehicles than their neighbours in the big company sector. It seems likely that this could be the case; after all, the municipal purse sometimes seemed bottomless when general managers wanted to add a few support vehicles to their fleets. It all contributed to municipal pride in having lots of vehicles in livery with the corporation crest on the side.

Inevitably the ancillary fleets grew in proportion to the main motorbus and trolleybus fleets. There were the vehicles that kept the buses running — the breakdown and tow wagons, the tower wagons to deal with overhead problems — and then came vans, for inspectors or for parcels, and the engineers needed vans and lorries to transport heavy items around the town. There were learner buses, their number often depending on the labour situation and the need for drivers — and of course normal service buses could be pressed into learner service.

There were staff canteens, often in town and city centres, where staff could relax over a 'cuppa' between duties. There were tree-loppers — cut-down double-deckers that allowed staff to keep trees on double-deck routes cut back to prevent tree damage (ie damage to the trees and to the buses, though not necessarily in that order of priority).

And of course there were the cars — a fine car for the general manager, a slightly lesser model for the more fortunate lower ranks of management — but these are not covered in this book.

The photographs in the book cover the period from the start of the 20th century through to the 1980s, by which time the shape of the municipal map had changed and the formation of the Passenger Transport Executives and the local government reorganisation of the 1970s meant that many authorities now traded under different names. As this is written, the once-significant proportion of the UK bus fleet that was in local authority control has been reduced from a peak, half a century ago, of over 20,000 buses operated by just under 100 undertakings, to the situation at the time of writing where just 17 undertakings operate around 2,800 buses.

The book concentrates on motorbus and trolleybus operations, but a few ancillary vehicles will be found on tramway duties. The first municipal transport ancillary vehicles were needed to keep the tramcar fleets going, and we set the scene with a series of 'works' trams.

There are three case histories, featuring ancillary vehicles in very different municipal fleets — Birmingham, Edinburgh and Huddersfield.

Many of the photographs for this book have come from the Ian Allan Library. Others have come from, in particular, David Harvey and Geoff Lumb; to these gentlemen I am very grateful.

Gavin Booth
Edinburgh
May 2001

5

Tramway service vehicles

Service vehicles could be found in most tramway fleets. These were typically older passenger cars that had been converted in the department's workshops, and were used in a variety of support rôles.

There were breakdown cars — predecessors of the motorbus recovery wagons — that headed off to rescue 'dead' tramcars, though the inherent inflexibility of the tramcar meant that it could be difficult to get close to the disabled tram; increasingly, tramway departments used motor vehicles for this work.

There were also the occasional trams with overhead towers, often for use on railway-type track, and those converted for specialist purposes — water cars to lay the dust, rail grinders, welding cars, salt cars, snowploughs and snowbrooms.

The majority, however, could be classed as works cars, which carried the permanent-way gangs out to attend to the tramlines. These acted as transport to the site of the work and as shelters where the gangs took their breaks, as well as carrying a range of necessary tools, equipment and other supplies. Much of the routine work to the permanent way and overhead was carried out at night after normal services had finished, or on Sunday mornings and other quieter times when the service car would not be required to move back and forth out of the way of cars in public service.

The works cars in the tramway fleets were the clear predecessors of the ancillary vehicles in the motorbus and trolleybus fleets, often performing similar functions — particularly the tower wagons and recovery vehicles. Typically, works trams were withdrawn from the passenger fleet and, because they clocked up fairly low mileages, outlasted their contemporaries, sometimes to go into preservation either as works cars or as the basis for restoration to original condition.

Below: **Aberdeen Corporation built this Emergency car in 1902 on a Brill 21E truck and used it to attend breakdowns and accidents on the system.** *W. A. Camwell*

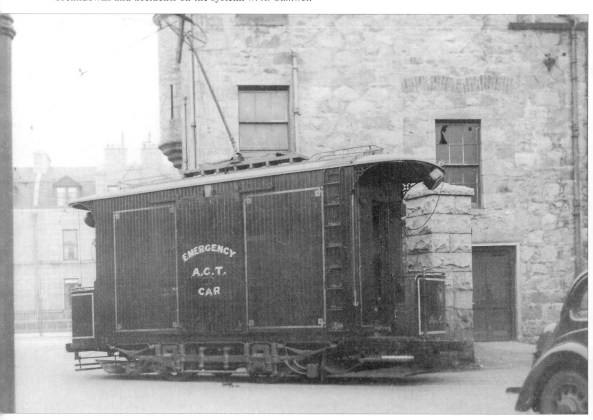

Above:
Blackpool overhead line car No 4, fitted with a collapsible platform, stands at Thornton Gate on 18 April 1949. This was originally 'Marton Box Car' No 31, built in 1901 and converted for departmental use in 1934. Later numbered 754, the tram was subsequently preserved and is now fully restored at Beamish. *Michael H. Waller*

Below:
One of the major uses for departmental trams was for the movement of stores. Leeds No R2 was, like the majority of the operator's stores cars, rebuilt from an older passenger tram, in this case BTH-built No 73A in 1937. It is pictured in City Square on 21 August 1949. *Michael H. Waller*

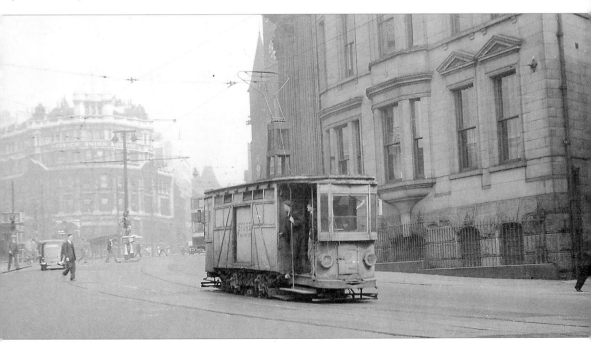

Above:

Sunderland was another operator that converted elderly passenger cars for departmental use. No B, seen here in May 1950 in Wheatsheaf depot towards the end of its life (it was scrapped the following year), was originally built in 1901 by Dick Kerr on a Brill 21E four-wheel truck. It received a top cover prior to 1916 and lower deck windscreens prior to World War 1. It was converted into a works car during the 1930s. *Michael H. Waller*

Below:

Although a number of tramway operators were involved in the movement of freight over their networks — such as coal in Huddersfield — there were few electric locomotives in the hands of tramway operators. One of these was in Blackpool, which acquired an English Electric locomotive in 1927 primarily for the movement of coal to Fleetwood power station. When this traffic ceased in 1949, the locomotive was used solely for permanent-way duties. Withdrawn in 1966 and subsequently preserved at the National Tramway Museum, it is seen here at Fleetwood depot on 9 September 1948. *Michael H. Waller*

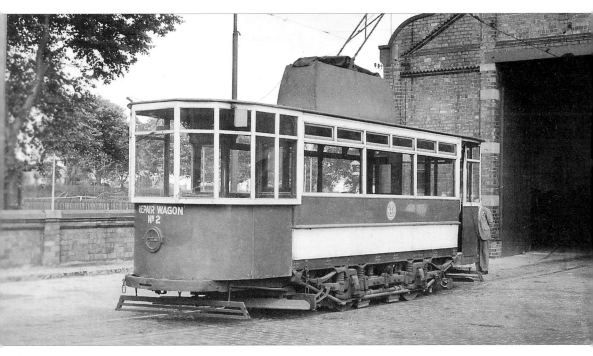

Above:
Dundee Corporation Repair Wagon No 2, converted in 1935 from a 1907 Brush-built double-decker on Brill 21E truck; it survived until 1956, the year the system closed. It is seen outside Maryfield Depot on 16 August 1950.
Michael H. Waller

Below:
Leeds No R2 again, this time at the Swinegate permanent-way yard on 18 September 1948. In the foreground is one of the PW Department's wagons, whilst to the left of the photograph can be seen a pile of setts; under the terms of the 1870 Tramways Act, tramway operators were responsible for the maintenance of the road surface to a distance of 18in beyond the outermost rail. This imposed a heavy burden upon tramway operators, particularly as other road users made use of the well-maintained section of road when much of the rest of the highway was unmade-up.
Michael H. Waller

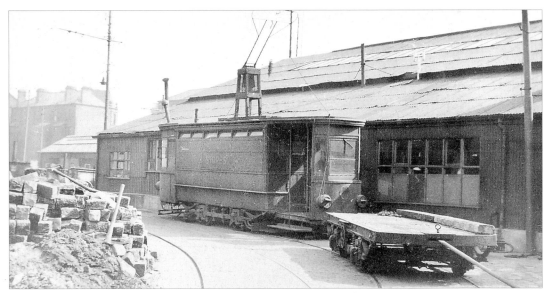

Above:
Pictured in its home depot on 9 October 1948, towards the end of the system's life, Bury No 1 was typical of many multi-rôle vehicles operated by the smaller municipalities in that it could serve as a rail grinder and water car. It was delivered as a purpose-built works car by Mountain & Gibson — appropriately a Bury-based company — in 1906.
Michael H. Waller

Left:
Another Leeds works car, No 4, is pictured at Swinegate PW yard on 18 September 1948. This was originally a tippler wagon, one of 22 built between 1906 and 1922 for the movement of sands, salts, etc. *Michael H. Waller*

Bottom right:
This former Reading Corporation horse-drawn tower wagon was acquired from the undertaking by the Reading Transport Society, now the British Trolleybus Society. It is seen in 1968. Although it appears crude, the tower wagon principle seems to have been established at an early stage, and it is recognisably a predecessor of future generations. *R. S. Brown*

Tower wagons

In the days of electric tramways and trolleybuses, tower wagons were among the most familiar municipal ancillary vehicles to be seen on the streets of Britain's towns and cities.

The earliest tramway tower wagons were horse-drawn, but as the motor vehicle developed in the early part of the 20th century, solid-tyred and later pneumatic-tyred vehicles were built. The need for a speedy response when there were problems with the overhead meant that pneumatic tyres were preferred, particularly on cobbled roads, but solid-tyred vehicles lasted for a surprisingly long time in some undertakings.

Some tower wagons were purpose-built vehicles, and others were conversions of motorbuses. Sometimes the tower itself outlasted various chassis.

In the days when the corporation transport department's workshop could turn its hand to producing a wide variety of vehicles, it was commonplace for the tower to be built in-house, and of course the buses were converted in-house too.

The tower itself was usually built of wood, and operated by hand, either with a screw-type lifting gear or a system of pulleys, which extended the tower, concertina-style, to a working height of around 20ft, suitable for working on overhead wiring or lamp-posts.

Some form of accommodation was necessary for the overhead maintenance crew. On the early examples it could be just a seat with a top cover; on later examples it was an extended cab, on pure commercial vehicles, or a section of bus body, on bus conversions.

As the photographs show, the bus conversions tended to

follow a similar pattern. The bus body would be cut away some two or three bays back, and closed off. The tower would be mounted above the rear axle, which suited weight distribution, and the rest of the chassis behind the rear axle would be cut away, resulting in a short 'tail'.

Tower wagons often doubled up as tow wagons, with facilities for a solid towbar to move disabled vehicles.

As tramway and trolleybus operations were replaced by motorbuses, the need for tower wagons reduced. Some were retained to handle street-lighting repairs and maintenance, and in seaside towns like Blackpool and Morecambe & Heysham they were used to help erect the municipal illuminations. Blackpool still, of course, has its municipal tramway, and a range of ancillary vehicles is still maintained.

Today's equivalent of the tower wagon is the extendable 'cherry-picker', which allows a greater degree of control and accuracy when handling wiring or street lighting.

Below:
Another early Daimler used as the basis for a tower wagon, although with rather less in the way of comforts for the crew. AK 2809 was supplied to Bradford Corporation Tramways in 1914.
Ian Allan Library

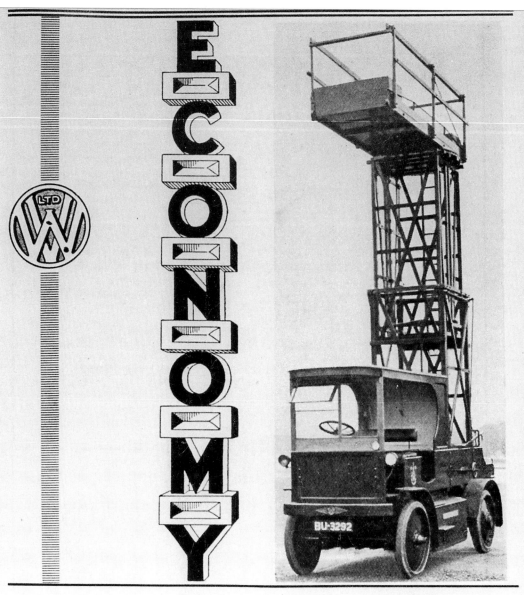

Walker Electric Tower Wagon supplied to the Oldham Corporation.

Walker Electric Inspection Wagons
REACH THE HEIGHT OF ECONOMY

WALKER VEHICLES
LIMITED,

Clare House, Kingsway, London, W.C. 2.

Left:
Battery-electric tower wagons were briefly popular in the 1920s. This contemporary advertisement shows a Walker supplied to Oldham Corporation, BU 3292. *G. Lumb collection*

Right
Another Walker electric tower wagon, a 2-ton vehicle for Liverpool Corporation, KC 5298. *G. Lumb collection*

Below right:
A 1924 Railless trolleybus with Short 36-seat body, West Hartlepool No 3 (EF 2123) poses beside the undertaking's tower wagon, based on the chassis of a 1914 former London General B-type double-deck bus, LH 8216 (B2766). *Ian Allan Library*

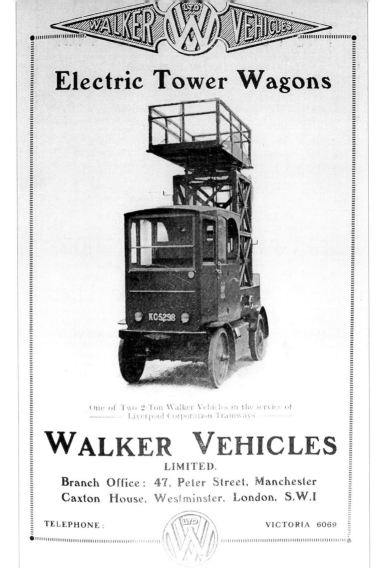

Electric Tower Wagons

KC5298

One of Two 2-Ton Walker Vehicles in the service of
Liverpool Corporation Tramways

WALKER VEHICLES
LIMITED.
Branch Office : 47, Peter Street, Manchester
Caxton House, Westminster, London, S.W.1

TELEPHONE :   VICTORIA 6069

Above:
Two Dundee Corporation 1927/8 Leyland Lion PLSC1 buses reconstructed as tower wagons Nos 1/2 for the city's tramway system in 1938. A contemporary press report describes how the Leyland bodywork was cut away for fitting of the tower directly over the rear axle. The remaining bodywork was fitted out with a bench and lockers. The oak two-section tower had a minimum height of 13ft 4in and a maximum height of 20ft 2in. The screw-type lifting gear, operated by hand from the rear of the vehicle through bevel gearing, was described as 'so light that one man can manipulate it quite easily'. *Ian Allan Library*

Top left:
Bournemouth Corporation started trolleybus operation in 1933, and its system was one of the last to close, in 1969. These two Tilling-Stevens TS6 motorbuses, RU 2013/4, were bought in 1925 and withdrawn a decade later for conversion to tower wagons Nos TW2/6. They are seen in 1948. *Alan B. Cross*

Left:
Used by Coventry Corporation for the maintenance of its tramway system, HP 450, an AEC YC new in 1919 with Hora body, is seen after conversion in the 1930s. *TravelLens*

Right:
Dating from 1911, this Leyland — note the splendid radiator badge — was still in use by Leicester during World War 2, as evidenced by the hooded headlamps.
D. R. Harvey collection

This secondhand 1928 Leyland PLSC Lion, UP 473, was in use as a tower wagon in 1951 in Darlington, with another tower wagon visible behind. Passing is No 56 (FHN 231), a 1939 Leyland TB5 with centre-entrance Brush body. Darlington bought only single-deck trolleybuses until 1949, when a short-lived batch of double-deckers arrived. Like Ipswich, Darlington bought its first motorbuses in 1950.
Alan B. Cross

Motorbuses often lasted well beyond their normal retirement date if they were converted to ancillary vehicles. Walsall Corporation DH 6421, a 1928 Dennis E with Vickers body, was withdrawn in 1937, converted to a tower wagon the following year, and was scrapped in 1960.
Ian Allan Library

Sitting in Don Everall's scrapyard in Wolverhampton in 1950 was DA 9032, a former Wolverhampton Corporation Tilling-Stevens TS6 which was new in 1925 with a Fleming single-deck bus body. It became tower wagon No 1 in 1933, and lasted in this form with the undertaking until 1947.
Alan B. Cross

Derby Corporation operated trolleybuses from 1932 until 1967 and used various former motorbuses from its fleet as the basis of tower wagons. No 1 (RC 2345) is a 1934 Crossley Alpha with Brush body, which was rebuilt as a tower wagon in 1944. It was withdrawn in 1958.
R. H. G. Simpson

Top left:

**An interesting conversion by
Nottingham City Transport —
AEC Regent bus TV 6749
converted to normal control and
fitted out as a tower wagon,
complete with trailer.**
G. Lumb collection

Bottom left:

**Derby tower wagon No 2
(RC 4252), photographed in 1966,
was a Daimler COG5 new in 1936
with a Brush double-deck body.**
Peter J. Relf

Right:

**A similar 1936 Daimler COG5,
Derby tower wagon No 3
(RC 4248) is seen in 1964 in
Market Place after the overhead
had been broken.** *T. W. Moore*

Below:

**A more unusual Derby tower
wagon, No 4 (ARC 267), was built
on a Tilling-Stevens B20 chassis
that had formerly been used by the
War Department as a searchlight
lorry. Acquired by Derby in 1948,
it was withdrawn in 1966.**
R. H. G. Simpson

Top left:
Flanked by two Guy Arab III single-deckers, Wolverhampton Corporation's DDA 882, a 1942 Fordson 7W tower wagon that was withdrawn in 1959. Guy Arab No 568, on the left, would serve as a snowplough for the corporation after withdrawal in 1960.
Alan D. Broughall

Centre left:
Wolverhampton supported local industry in its motorbus and trolleybus fleet, and this 1947 Guy Vixen tower wagon, No 8 (EUK 771), seen outside Cleveland Road garage, was also locally built.
S. N. J. White

Bottom left:
Wolverhampton JW 5792 was a Daimler COG5, new in 1934 with Park Royal body, which was withdrawn in 1942 and the chassis used for tower wagon No 6. In this form it was used from 1945 until 1962. *Roy Marshall*

Top right:
Photographed at Blackness in 1954, Dundee Corporation tower wagon TW2 (YJ 4104) was a 1937 Daimler COG5 with Cowieson body, converted after withdrawal in 1951. *Michael H. Waller*

Bottom right:
Blackpool Corporation used its former motorbus No 6 (FV 9043) as tower wagon No 240 between 1957 and 1964. It was a Leyland Tiger TS7 with distinctive fully-fronted Burlingham bodywork. In Blackpool, like other seaside towns with illuminations, these were used for more than just overhead wire duties. Note the mirror above the driver's cab trained on the tower. Sister vehicle FV 9044 passed into preservation. *Alan B. Cross*

Right:

Manchester Corporation was an early user of VHF radio to communicate with its vehicles. This Thornycroft tower wagon, HVM 93, was fitted with a radio in 1950, and was directed to emergency situations by the central control point. The aerial is just visible on the roof above the driver's cab. *Ian Allan Library*

Below:

Before the final closure of the Reading trolleybus system on 3 November 1968, trial runs were carried out using the Corporation's AEC Mercury tower wagon and the buses which would take part in the final procession. Trolleybus No 144 (DRD 130), a 1949 BUT 9611T/Park Royal, made the final journey, and is now preserved. *Michael Bennett*

The trolleypoles are stretched as Walsall Corporation trolleybus No 857 (TDH 907) negotiates overhead repairs being carried out by the crew of AEC Mercury TXV 906 on the 15 route in Coalpool Lane. New in 1955, trolleybus 857 was one of the ground-breaking Sunbeam F4As with 70-seat Willowbrook bodies bought in 1954/5 — the first 30ft-long two-axle buses permitted to run in Britain, paving the way for relaxed regulations in 1956. *D. R. Harvey collection*

Cardiff Corporation tower wagon No 2 (KG 8904) was a 1936 Leyland Titan TD4c with Northern Counties double-deck body that was converted in 1949 and lasted until 1961. *D. A. Thompson*

Above:
A purpose-built tower wagon for Leeds City Transport on Bedford OL chassis. *Ian Allan Library*

Left:
Delivered during World War 2, Edinburgh Corporation's tower wagon No 2 (DWS 528) was a 1944 Austin three-tonner which may well have inherited an older tower. *Gavin Booth collection*

Above:

A fine bonneted AEC Mammoth, AWB 368, used by Sheffield Corporation as a tower wagon.
G. Lumb collection

Left:

This photo appeared in the transport trade press in 1948 to publicise Sheffield Corporation's move to two-way radio communication 'to ease traffic control arrangements and repair facilities'. Tower wagon No 5 shown, based on AEC Regent bus BWA 830, was to be fitted with the radio system to keep delays to a minimum. In addition, the 'man on the top' was able to communicate with the driver by using a GEC hand microphone, as he is demonstrating here.
Ian Allan Library

Left:
Left:
The driver of ex-Huddersfield AEC Regent VH 6217, converted to a tower wagon, watches as de-wired Bournemouth Corporation No 239 (KLJ 339), a 1950 BUT 9641T with Weymann 56-seat dual-door, twin-staircase body, blocks the traffic. VH 6217 passed into preservation. *D. R. Harvey collection*

Bottom left:
Still supporting local industry, Wolverhampton Corporation purchased Guy Warrior tower wagon No 1 (WDA 301), new in 1958. *S. N. J. White*

Top right:
Walsall opted for lighter-weight tower wagons in later years. This is 706 BDH, a 1957 Karrier Bantam. *D. R. Harvey collection*

Below:
Walsall's 268 FDH, a 1959 Dennis Stork with crew accommodation. Note the mirror above the driver's position. *D. R. Harvey collection*

Above:
The crew of Bradford Corporation Karrier Gamecock CK3 tower wagon FKW 973 attend to overhead repairs as trolleybus No 588 (HNU 827), a 1941 ex-Notts & Derby AEC 661T/Weymann bought by Bradford in the 1950s, edges past. *D. R. Harvey collection*

Left:
The 'cherry-picker' replaced the more basic tower wagon technology. Morecambe & Heysham Corporation 1947 AEC Regent II GTJ 694, originally with Park Royal double-deck body, is seen in June 1972 in use by the department of the local authority responsible for the resort's illuminations. It is now preserved. *M. Fowler*

Above:
**Blackpool's famous seaside
tramway from Starr Gate to
Fleetwood still needs specialist
support vehicles. This 'maid of all
work' Unimog Zweiweg, YFV 577Y,
No 440 in the fleet, was designed to
run on rails as well as on the road.
It doubles as a tower wagon and
permanent-way sweeper, and can
also tow trams, as demonstrated
here with 'Balloon' car No 710.**
Ian Allan Library

Right:
**A fine study of a tower wagon in
action, though almost certainly not
one destined for a British municipal
fleet. An Albion CX2 dating from
the late 1930s, it is posed
somewhere in Glasgow, but its
customer is likely to have been
overseas, possibly in South Africa.**
Ian Allan Library

Recovery vehicles

The vehicles that any municipal general manager or chief engineer worth his salt would not wish to see on the streets are the recovery vehicles. A broken-down motorbus or trolleybus is not a good advertisement for a transport undertaking, but the presence of a tow wagon at the scene of a breakdown only serves to draw attention to the problem. The worst-case scenario is a broken-down bus being towed along the High Street in the middle of the evening rush hour.

There are chief engineers who have issued instructions that tow wagons are only to be used in the direst emergencies. Many would rather send out a discreet van with a couple of mechanics to try to sort the problem *in situ*. Others will leave a broken-down bus at the roadside until the streets are quieter before despatching the tow wagon to bring it in.

There was a time when the 'spanner and hammer' school of vehicle engineering could cure most ills on the spot. Today's more sophisticated buses, bristling with electronics, will 'sit down' if there is the slightest problem; in previous generations, an experienced driver would have a good idea what was wrong if his bus started to play up, and could nurse it to the terminus or garage, or could even sort it himself.

Tow wagons usually had a crane mounted over the rear axle, though in practice this was used for more major incidents when buses turned on to their sides or had to be rescued from an awkward situation. For straightforward towing work where a bus was still essentially intact, a solid towbar was often used.

Many municipalities chose to convert buses into tow wagons, leaving the forward part of the body intact to provide accommodation for maintenance staff and some of their equipment. Some mounted a crane behind this compartment, while others left this area open and relied on towbars.

The equipment carried on recovery vehicles allowed staff to carry out many types of repair on the spot. Typically there would be various jacks, fire extinguishers, emergency lighting, saws, hammers, blocks, etc, as well as a workbench and vice. Roof-mounted searchlights provided extra illumination, and extra batteries were often carried.

For many municipalities, as with many other bus operators, the AEC Matador proved to be the ideal basis for recovery vehicles. During and immediately after World War 2, AEC built over 9,000 four-wheel-drive Matador O853 'medium artillery tractors' for the War Department. When these became surplus to WD requirements, bus

This fine sequence of photos shows what a typical recovery vehicle was all about. Bury Corporation EN 4501 started life in 1930 as Leyland Titan TD1 double-deck bus No 21 and in 1946 became recovery vehicle No 202. The interior views are particularly interesting, showing the seating area for the recovery crew, the workbench and vice, hammers, shovel, rope, saws, fire extinguishers, lamps — all necessary on a well-equipped recovery wagon.
G. Lumb collection

operators and recovery specialists snapped them up, and many are still around over half a century later.

With a rear-mounted crane, a Matador could be simply converted for civilian use, but bus-company engineers have always tended to take a pride in 'their' vehicles, and many were extensively rebuilt and modernised in the course of their careers, often using bus body parts that would be in stock in the stores. Rather as fire tenders are lovingly looked after by the fire crews, recovery vehicles were 'personalised' by the engineering staff and, although their presence was rarely needed in some fleets, were always in top mechanical condition, ready to dash off to rescue a bus, orange lights a-flashing.

Created in the period 1969-74, the PTEs sometimes turned to impressive new recovery trucks for their bus fleets, which in a couple of cases exceeded 2,000 vehicles.

Today, while some bus companies still have their own recovery vehicles, others increasingly rely on commercial facilities.

Left:
Preston Corporation's recovery vehicle was this modified Leyland Titan PD1, here at the depot in 1973 after repainting into the undertaking's blue and ivory livery in place of its previous all-brown scheme. *P. J. Hesketh*

Below:
Swan Street, Leicester, in March 1946 after an accident involving Corporation No 286 (JF 5889), a 1934 Leyland Titan TD3 with MCCW body. Attending it is JF 5005, a 1933 Crossley Condor breakdown lorry, formerly a double-deck bus. The TD3 was withdrawn after the accident, but the breakdown lorry soldiered on until 1951. *D. R. Harvey collection*

Above:
Passenger Transport Journal in November 1942 included this photo of
'An Interesting Conversion' of a Nottingham City Transport bus as a
breakdown wagon. 'In these days of short supply the ingenuity of general
managers and engineers is being tested to full in finding new uses for
obsolescent equipment,' the article read. 'Not only are old bus chassis being
used as a basis for technical equipment, but complete single-deck buses are
being converted for such diverse purposes as mobile canteens, chapels,
cinemas and even, in some cases, as dormitories. In every phase of
industrial and transport activity we are learning to assess scrap material,
equipment, chassis and bodies, at a new and higher value, and this re-
assessment of values might very well be of permanent benefit. No doubt
there will be a certain amount of backsliding when the present emergency
passes but, even so, a substantial residue of economy will certainly remain.'
Against this background Nottingham had converted a petrol-engined AEC
Regent with a body adapted for mounting an 8-ton Harvey Frost fully-
swivelling crane over the rear axle. The compartment at the rear of the
driver's cab contained the breakdown equipment — jacks, bars, packings,
emergency lamps, saws, hammers and drifts. *Ian Allan Library*

Below left:
Passenger Transport in May 1944
featured this Leigh Corporation
conversion of a Leyland Lion LT2
into a breakdown wagon. The body
has been cut back to the second
bay behind the entrance, and the
whole vehicle has been shortened
behind the rear axle. Here a
crossmember was welded and
fitted with a towing jaw. A sliding
door in the rear wall of what
remains of the body allows access
to the lorry portion. To prevent
wheelspin, the rear wheelarches
were boxed in and the cavities
filled with concrete, approximately
half a ton of 'ballast' being added
in this way. In the crew cabin was
a comprehensive range of
equipment, including a small
bench with vice, various-sized
jacks and a series of fire
extinguishers. A swivelling
spotlight was fitted on the rear
dome — though the white-edged
mudguards and hooded headlamps
remind us that this was wartime,
and the spotlight may not have
been used too often in its early
days. *Ian Allan Library*

Above:
This splendid early-1920s solid-tyred, normal-control Karrier tow wagon survived intact for many years in Stockport Corporation's garage, and is now preserved.
J. J. Holmes

Left:
Portsmouth Corporation's TW2, a significantly shortened Leyland Titan TD2 tow wagon.
Ian Allan Library

Above:

Towing of a different kind. This 1931 photo shows Nottingham Corporation No 37 (later registered TV 4475), a new Ransomes, Sims & Jefferies D6 trolleybus with Brush 60-seat body on delivery on a solid tow behind a French-built Chernard-Walcker drawbar tractor. Of course, unlike motorbuses, trolleybuses could not normally be delivered under their own power, so arrangements like this had to be made. At least the Brush coachworks at Loughborough was not too far from Nottingham. *Ian Allan Library*

Right:

Built in the 1940s, like so many that were later acquired for recovery work, Leicester City Transport acquired this AEC Matador in 1964; No 1 (on tradeplates 395 BC) is seen at Abbey Park Road depot in April 1979. *Mike Greenwood*

Bottom right:

In 1948 Barrow Corporation converted this prewar Leyland Titan into a breakdown vehicle, largely using apprentice labour. A heavy-duty 10-ton crane was fitted as well as a towing pole 'of a special type developed by London Transport'. A towing trailer was also part of the vehicle's equipment. *Ian Allan Library*

Left:
Southport Corporation placed this four-wheel-drive AEC Matador in service in 1952. Based on an ex-War Department vehicle, it had a Harvey Frost 6-ton crane mounted on its own sub-chassis in order to give the necessary clearance to permit the use of the standard 14in x 20in tyres desired for sand operation — a feature required because of the undertaking's famous Southport–Ainsdale Shore service. The body was built by the transport department and incorporated a covered workshop and a large-capacity tool locker seat. An amplifier with loudspeakers allowed the use of a wandering microphone, so the person in charge of towing or winching could direct the driver's actions without fear of misinterpretation by signalling.
Ian Allan Library

Below:
Doncaster Corporation's towing vehicle, a cut-back Leyland Tiger with Leyland body, DT 7615, tows Doncaster's last trolleybus, No 375 (CDT 636), a 1945 Sunbeam W with 1950s Roe body, now preserved, to the trolleybus museum at Sandtoft in 1964. *M. Fowler*

Above:

How many Bournemouth Corporation employees does it take to change a wheel on a trolleybus? Four, from the evidence of this 1961 photo, though one is an inspector and another appears to be the driver. Guy Arab I FRU 180, new in 1943 with Park Royal double-deck bodywork, seen after conversion to a towing lorry and running on tradeplates 094 EL, is in attendance as running repairs are carried out on No 255 (KLJ 355), a 1950 BUT 9641T with Weymann bodywork. *Gavin Booth*

Below:

A Manchester Corporation AEC Matador mobile crane tows trolleybus No 1174 (GNA 92), a 1942 Crossley TDD4 with Crossley-MCCW body, at Ardwick Green in April 1960. *P. J. Thompson*

Above:

Preserved Bradford (ex-St Helens) No 799 (BDJ 87), a 1951 BUT 9611T/East Lancs, returns to St Helens in September 1969 behind PDJ 936F, an ex-WD AEC Matador that was in the St Helens fleet between 1968 and 1974. *P. J. Thompson*

Below:

When the Wolverhampton trolleybus system closed on 5 March 1967, buses that were not needed for the last day's service were driven away from the Cleveland Road depot to the local scrap merchant. No 443 (EJW 443), a 1947 Sunbeam W with 1960 Roe body, is towed away behind the corporation's Karrier wagon. *T. W. Moore*

Above:
**Leicester's 1975 Ford D1210 breakdown vehicle No 2
attends 1966 Leyland Titan PD3A/1 No 53 (GRY 53D)
with MCCW bodywork, in Charles Street in July 1980.**
Mike Greenwood

Below:
**Glasgow Corporation converted its AEC Matadors in
the 1960s, largely using bus parts. The windscreen and
dome, it will be noted, are those of the contemporary
Alexander-bodied Leyland Atlanteans.** *Alan Millar*

Above:
Cardiff Bus used this 1981 ERF B-series, NUT 344W, as its breakdown/towing vehicle in the 1980s. *T. S. Powell*

Below:
This splendid bonneted AEC Majestic, new in 1970 and numbered RV1 in the Derby fleet, was previously registered VTC 733H and was acquired from Wreckers International in 1976, being used on Derby's tradeplates 040 CH. It is seen in January 1982, during the heaviest snowfall for more than 30 years, rescuing Daimler Fleetline FE30AGR/Alexander No 53 (NAL 53P), which had been involved in a collision. *D. J. Stanier*

Above:
Hyndburn's 1949 Guy Arab tow wagon, No 10 (formerly KTC 615, but on tradeplates 0707 B) sits in wait in August 1981, perhaps expecting problems with the undertaking's Seddon RU with rare Seddon coach body, No 38 (STC 986M). *M. Fowler*

Right:
A closer view of Hyndburn's No 10, with Guy rear-entrance bodywork. It was new in 1949 to Hyndburn's predecessor, Accrington Corporation, and enjoyed a long career. KTC 615 survives in preservation.
John Robinson

Left:
Used by Blackburn as a recovery vehicle, No 506 (ETF 484F), an East Lancs-bodied Leyland Titan PD2A/37, looks like a normal member of the bus fleet, except for the locker on the nearside for housing spare wheels.
Michael Dryhurst

Below:
Nottingham's last trolleybus, No 506 (KTV 506), a 1949 BUT 9641T with Brush body, is moved using a David Brown Selectamatic 1200 farm tractor. This bus is now preserved.
Ian Allan Library

Left:
**Kingston-upon-Hull's recovery
vehicle in 1984 was this Ford
Custom Cab DA2214, running on
tradeplates 703 AT. It lived in
Lombard Street depot, adjacent to
Ferensway bus station.** *G. B. Wise*

Below:
**Basic Matador. Surprisingly
unmodified, Brighton's AEC
Matador tow wagon at Lewes
Road garage in April 1973.**
W. T. Cansick

Above:
Another basic Matador — West Bromwich No 51, on tradeplates 15 AEA, in Oak Lane garage yard. *R. Weaver*

Below:
Still with its original cab, West Midlands PTE No 170, on tradeplates 5127 O, was an ex-RAF AEC Matador which passed to the PTE from Wolverhampton Corporation. *D. R. Harvey collection*

Above:
**Grimsby-Cleethorpes' towing vehicle TBE 537T
(though running on tradeplates 050 EE), an Atkinson
38-tonner with Rolls-Royce Eagle III engine, acquired
in 1983.** *G. B. Wise*

Below:
**Merseyside PTE's Wirral Division breakdown tender
in 1977 was this yellow-liveried Leyland Titan PD2/37
with Massey body, seen in Birkenhead. It was new to
Birkenhead Corporation in 1969.** *R. L. Wilson*

Above:
Adapted with Alexander Y-type parts, Greater Manchester Transport's AEC Matador recovery vehicle No A45 leaves Victoria Park, Warrington, after a rally in May 1977. *M. F. Haddon*

Below:
An impressive-looking ERF recovery vehicle supplied to Merseyside PTE. *Ian Allan Library*

Below right:
On driver-training duty in the late 1930s, Coventry Corporation's No 51 (VC 6518), a 1930 Maudslay ML7 with 60-seat Brush body that was withdrawn in 1939. A bus like this doubtless sorted the men from the boys. *TravelLens*

Driver-training vehicles

In days of full employment, municipal bus undertakings would often get by with just one dedicated driver-training vehicle; indeed some would just detail a bus from the service fleet. But as the staff turnover rate increased and operators faced staff shortages, the 'learner' fleet would often increase dramatically.

Bus operators often had to train drivers from scratch; some prospective drivers had never even driven a private car. It took a leap of faith on the part of the transport department and its driving instructors to allow new recruits out on the road in an 8-ton bus, yet that was the way it worked. Some hedged their bets by having dual controls, allowing the instructor to rescue a potentially dangerous situation. Others eschewed this, but sometimes mounted an emergency brake within easy reach.

It was essential for the instructor to communicate with the driver, which in the days of half-cab buses could be done by a sliding window in the bulkhead behind the driver or, in more permanent conversions, removal of part of the bulkhead. With the driving position often at a higher level than the lower-deck seating, a raised platform allowed the instructor to watch the road as well as the pupil.

Municipal undertakings were not great believers in giving their trainee drivers an easy time. The view was usually taken that if drivers could handle the most difficult buses in the fleet, they could handle anything. Coupled to this were the regulations that required drivers to take their tests on buses with a clutch and manual gearbox if they required a licence allowing them to drive all types of bus and coach. At one stage it was possible to pass a test on a bus with an automatic gearbox — and that included preselective gearboxes as well as semi-automatics — and your licence allowed you to drive only these buses.

For many years, the vehicles on which drivers took their PSV tests dictated the licence they held and the vehicles they were legally permitted to drive. This meant that a test taken on a single-decker with an automatic gearbox only permitted you to drive similar vehicles. The same went for 'automatic' double-deckers and, indeed, for single-deckers with 'proper' gearboxes.

The 'all types' licence, awarded after tuition and a test on a manual-gearbox double-decker, was the most attractive and flexible PSV licence to hold, and there are still undertakings today with staff trained and passed-out on automatics where drivers with all-types licences are prized because they can drive vehicles like coaches — or, indeed, historic vehicles — with 'proper' gearboxes.

Then somebody realised that a few feet of metal above the driver was in most cases less important than a few feet of metal between the axles, say, or at the rear overhang. A driver could legitimately pass the test on a 27ft-long manual-'box double-decker and immediately step into the

driving seat of a 39ft 4in-long single-decker, with potentially embarrassing results. So height ceased to be a consideration, and now drivers must take their tests on single-deck buses at least 9m (29ft 6in) long.

In the past, drivers had to wrestle with some of the most unforgiving gearboxes and heavy steering on training buses. Even though buses with easy synchromesh gearboxes were perfectly acceptable, fleets that didn't include these — or perhaps where the management took the view that driving tuition should prepare you for everything — would use (or even specially buy) Bristols or Guys, which traditionally had some of the most difficult controls to master.

For a time, municipal learner buses were painted in fleet livery, with little more than an 'L' plate to signify what they were used for. Then some undertakings chose to paint them in distinctive schemes, either to prevent passengers from flagging them down, or (perhaps) to give adequate warning to other road users that the driver was a novice. These liveries were sometimes variations of the normal scheme, and sometimes totally different colours — often yellow — to provide a degree of visibility in busy urban streets. Some were even sensibly used to promote bus driving as a career — 'Drive a Bus with Us'.

As newer vehicles were adapted for driver training, it became necessary to carry out more fundamental conversion work. With a rear entrance, there was no problem: the driving instructor sat right behind the pupil. But on a forward-entrance double-decker there was a staircase in the way, and this would be removed — usually after removing the upper-deck seats — and a raised seat provided where the stairwell had been. Where the solid stair panel had been, a window was usually put in. On a front-entrance double-decker there was space alongside the driver, though sometimes an alternative doorway was created, or the existing centre exit doors became the entrance.

On trolleybuses it was often possible for the instructor to perch to the left of the driver in the empty space ahead of the front bulkhead.

Above:

Flanked by newer buses — a 1961 Daimler CVG6/Alexander on the left and a 1957 AEC Regent V/Park Royal on the right — Aberdeen Corporation No 111 (RG 8111), a 1937 Daimler COG6/Weymann, became a driver trainer on withdrawal in 1958, lasting in this guise until replaced by a 1945 Daimler CWD6. *F. McCallum*

Above left:

Bought by Derby Corporation from Coventry Corporation in 1949, this 1940 Daimler COG5/40 with Park Royal body, EVC 244, is seen in use as a driver trainer, Derby No 47. It is now preserved. *D. R. Harvey collection*

Left:

Older buses were often earmarked for driver-training duties, like Pontypridd UDC No 16 (ETX 322), a 1940 Bristol L5G with BBW body, seen as a trainer after its service life. *R. H. G. Simpson*

Right:

The prize for the lowest fleetnumber applied to a bus could well go to Coventry's No 00 (FHP 19), a 1948 Daimler CVA6 with MCCW body that became a trainer after withdrawal in 1966, and survived in this rôle until 1968. It is seen in Coventry's Pool Meadow bus station.

D. R. Harvey collection

Left:
There is no question that Blackpool BFR 366, a 1940 Leyland Titan TD5 with Burlingham fully-fronted centre-entrance body, is a Trainee Vehicle. It carried out these duties between 1957 and 1962. *R. H. G. Simpson*

Below:
Trolleybus drivers needed to be trained too. Bradford No 612 (KY 8215), a 1934 AEC 661T with 1944 Brush utility body, is seen on learner duties shortly before withdrawal in 1958.
D. R. Harvey collection

**A more permanent learner in
Bradford was No 062 (EKU 743),
a 1949 BUT 9611T with Roe
bodywork, parked in the town
centre in August 1967. It is now
preserved.** *P. K. Williamson*

Right:
**Walsall Corporation No 873
(HBE 542) acting as a more
discreet learner bus. It was a 1951
Crossley Empire TDD42/3 with
Roe body, new to Cleethorpes and
bought from Grimsby-Cleethorpes
in 1961, following the closure of
that trolleybus system.**
Ian Allan Library

When this photograph was taken, Darlington Corporation had an all-single-deck service fleet but still retained this 1964 Roe-bodied Daimler CCG5 (constant-mesh gearbox), AHN 455B, for driver-training purposes. It subsequently passed into preservation.
Michael Dryhurst

Brighton Corporation's No 74 (WCD 74), a 1959 Leyland Titan PD2/37 with four-bay Weymann Orion-style bodywork, seen at Lewes Road garage in September 1971 as a permanent driver-training bus. *M. Ovenden*

Below:
An unusual choice as a trainer was MKH 81. This ex-East Yorkshire 1951 Leyland Titan PD2/12 with full-front Roe Beverley Bar roof profile body, is seen as Halifax No 403 leaving Todmorden bus station in June 1972 on driver-training duties. *C. B. Golding*

Above:
Some municipal undertakings bought buses from other operators for use as training vehicles. Lincoln City Transport No 99 (CJN 441C), a 1965 Leyland Titan PD3/6 with Massey body, was new to Southend. Now preserved, it is seen at Sandtoft in 1989. *M. Fowler*

Above right:
Well, nobody said learning to drive a bus was going to be easy! Rhymney Valley driver trainer No 82 (422 CAX), a now-preserved 1961 AEC Regent V/Massey lowbridge, fights through the snow. It started life with one of Rhymney Valley's predecessors, the tiny Bedwas & Machen UDC. *Ian Allan Library*

Right:
Sunderland Corporation bought buses from Edinburgh Corporation for driver-training work. No 241 (NSF 901), a 1955 Guy Arab IV with Alexander body, had been a driver trainer in Edinburgh before passing to Sunderland in 1972. *S. N. Cowley*

Another Edinburgh bus to pass to Sunderland as a driver trainer was LFS 410, a 1954 Leyland Titan PD2/20/MCCW Orion. It passed into Tyneside PTE ownership with the Sunderland undertaking in 1973, becoming DT6 in 1974.
I. Hope

Edinburgh's own training fleet in the mid-1970s comprised a number of MCCW-bodied Leyland Titan PD2/20s from the large fleet bought for tram replacement. Lothian Region Transport No T13 (OFS 798), new in 1957, is seen in 1977 at King's Road, Portobello. This bus is now undergoing a very thorough restoration.
M. F. Haddon

Left:
The last rear-entrance bus of the former Wigan Corporation fleet to survive with Greater Manchester Transport was No 3200 (DJP 754), a 1958 Leyland Titan PD2/30 with locally-built Northern Counties body. Seen on driver-training work in Wallgate, Wigan, it has since passed into preservation.
John Robinson

Below:
Cardiff Corporation was still using this Bristol K6A with rebuilt Park Royal utility body, CKG 582, as a learner-driver vehicle in 1962, when it was photographed at Cardiff bus station.
Gavin Booth

Left:
Sitting at Burnley bus station between duties, Burnley & Pendle No 63 (ACW 645), a 1949 Leyland Titan PD2/1 with Leyland bodywork, new to the former Burnley, Colne & Nelson Joint Transport Committee, and now preserved. *Adrian A. Thomas*

Below left:
Two buses from former municipal fleets that had passed into West Yorkshire PTE in use as driver trainers. No 355 (KWX 17) is a 1951 all-Leyland Titan PD2/12 that was new to Todmorden JOC and passed to WYPTE via Calderdale JOC. In the background is No 3074 (DCP 74D), a former Halifax Leyland Titan PD2/37 with Weymann forward-entrance body. *D. R. Wootton*

Right:
Leicester FJF 199, a 1950 all-Leyland Titan PD2/12, as training vehicle No 301. *Kendon Photos*

Below:
Later Leicester trainers, Nos 400/1 (TBC 162/3), 1958 Leyland Titan PD3/1s with Park Royal bodywork, seen in Abbey Park Road depot. They joined the training fleet in 1974 and were withdrawn from this work in 1981. TBC 163 is now preserved. *Ian Allan Library*

Left:
**RDB 866, a 1961 AEC Reliance
2MU3RA with Willowbrook body,
new to North Western Road Car,
seen in use as training vehicle
TV13 in the SELNEC PTE fleet at
Hyde Road, Manchester, in
October 1974.** *M. S. Stokes*

Below left:
**In the 1970s operators tended to
make their training vehicles rather
more distinctive. No 10 in the
Wirral Division of Merseyside PTE
was FBG 910, a 1958 Massey-
bodied Leyland Titan PD2/40 new
to Birkenhead Corporation.
Photographed in February 1975
near Birkenhead Park, it wore a
special dark green and cream
training livery. It is now preserved.**
R. L. Wilson

Right:
**New in 1958 to Merthyr Tydfil
Corporation, this Leyland Titan
PD3/4 with East Lancs body had
become Lancaster's training bus
No 9841 (HB 9841) by the time it
was photographed in the early
1980s, but also doubled as a flood
warning vehicle for Morecambe
promenade.** *T. W. W. Knowles*

Below right:
**An attractive bus used by Derby
City Transport as a training
vehicle, No 395 (PFN 852), a 1959
AEC Regent V with fully-fronted
Park Royal body. It was painted in
the then current Blue Bus Services
livery, and was nicknamed
'The Puffin' on account of its
registration.** *D. J. Stanier*

Left:
Another view of Derby's ex-East Kent Regent, showing that the upper-deck seats have been removed — as indeed has the staircase. Where the staircase once was there is an elevated seat for the driving instructor, who has his own window, complete with sliding panels for hand signals, and an extra mirror. *M. Fowler*

Below:
A fine line-up of SELNEC driver-training vehicles at Stockport in the early 1970s. The two buses in the centre are ex-Ribble 1955 Leyland Titan PD2/13s with MCCW Orion bodies, HCK 464 and HRN 38, flanked by ex-Stockport 1960 PD2/30s PJA 919/8 with Longwell Green bodies. *Ian Allan Library*

Left:
More prominently lettered, Greater Manchester No 6628 (NBN 436), a 1959 Leyland Titan PD3/4 with forward-entrance East Lancs body formerly in the Bolton Corporation fleet and seen in Bolton in 1976. It is now preserved. *C. B. Golding*

Above:
Grampian Regional Transport, successor to Aberdeen Corporation, bought this 1963 ex-Greater Glasgow Leyland Atlantean PDR1/1 with Alexander body in 1976 purely for driver-training duties. No 91 (SGD 727) replaced a Daimler CVG6. *Alan Millar*

Below:
Away from its home base, Cleveland Transit No H12 (EPT 912B), a 1964 Leyland Atlantean/Park Royal, stands in Darlington while a United Auto Bristol REMH6G/Plaxton coach passes on National Express service to London, in September 1981. *Kevin Lane*

This page:

Another Cleveland Transit Leyland Atlantean/Park Royal, H18 (NPT 218D), dating from 1966, at Cargo Fleet on a grey day in July 1982. *Kevin Lane*

Top right:

Normal-height and low-height types compared at Derby. On the left is Derby training vehicle LB1 (KRC 175D), a 1966 Daimler Fleetline CRG6LX with Roe body, sitting alongside a very early Leyland Atlantean PDR1/1 with lowheight Weymann bodywork — No 63 (RTH 639), bought from City of Oxford in 1976 but new to James, Ammanford, in 1959. *Geoffrey W. Girling*

Bottom right:

The driver of this 1959 Greater Glasgow PTE Leyland Titan PD2/24 with Alexander-style Glasgow Corporation body, No L108 (SGD 10), may not have passed his test. L108 had passed to the training school in 1974 but was deroofed the following year, after which it was returned to the bus fleet proper, though normally used for publicity purposes. It has since been re-registered HSK 953, and now operates for Mac Tours in Edinburgh. *J. T. Park*

Lorries

In addition to the requirement for specialist tower and recovery vehicles, municipal bus undertakings often needed vehicles for more mundane duties. Simply transporting heavy equipment between garages and workshops, for instance, dictated the need for a works lorry.

Fewer of these were bus conversions, as platform lorries were easy to obtain, new or secondhand. In the early days of the 20th century, buses routinely doubled up as lorries, swapping bodies at weekends, for instance. But as buses became more sophisticated, this option was not available, and so purpose-built lorries were bought. These might be simple platform lorries, or perhaps tippers for use in road mending. Some were simply runabouts for the maintenance staff, while others had more specific purposes — pole carriers for lighting and traction poles, or rail-movers with trailers in connection with tramway systems.

Below:

Bradford Corporation started trolleybus operation on 20 June 1911 — the same day the Leeds system was inaugurated. Bradford's first two trolleybuses were Railless ET models with bodywork by Hurst Nelson, and No 502 (AK 8090) was converted to a trolley-battery lorry in 1916; its sister was converted later. No 502 lasted in this form until 1926.
G. Lumb collection

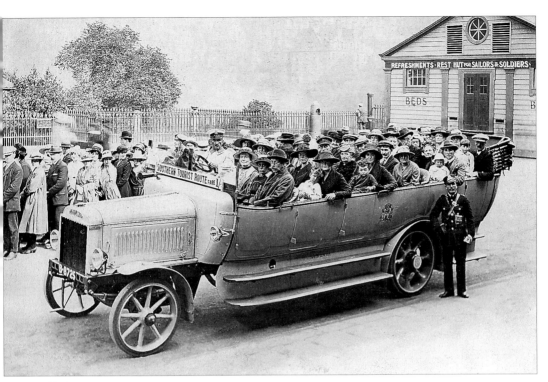

Above and below:

Early motorbus chassis were often convertible — used as lorries during the week and buses at weekends. Edinburgh Corporation did something slightly different with its 1919 Leyland N charabanc No 1 (B 8725), which is seen here in its normal guise about to set off on a local tour from The Mound; converted as a lorry, it was used to fetch coal from colliery sidings during the 1919 railway strike. No 1 later (in 1931) became a Transport Department lorry. *Gavin Booth collection*

Above:

In the background of this record of a World War 2 first-aid exercise is Leicester's No 44 (RY 7851), a Guy B, new in 1929 with a Brush bus body, withdrawn in 1939 and converted to a permanent-way lorry. It is seen in December 1941.

D. R. Harvey collection

Below:

This 1943 ex-WD Chevrolet was bought in 1946 by Leicester City Transport and registered EBC 228 for use as a permanent-way lorry. *P. Newland*

**This Belfast Corporation lorry
started life as 1942 Bedford OWB
with SMT utility bus body No 144
(GZ 962) and became lorry L65 in
1951. It was converted by the
Corporation to a unit wagon with
gantry with a Bedford-style cab,
and is seen in 1954, preparing to
tow new trolleybus No 234,
(OZ 7336), a 1952 BUT 9641T,
from the Harkness coachworks.**
W. H. Montgomery

Right:
**Portsmouth Corporation No 74
(RV 720) was a 1931 Crossley
Condor/Short double-decker
converted to a van/lorry.
It survives in preservation.**
Ian Allan Library

This fine Leyland six-wheeler, TS 9841 on tradeplates 091 TS, was still in use with Dundee Corporation in the mid-1950s. It is passing the city's main terminal point, in Dock Street. *Ian Allan Library*

The original caption on this photo reads: 'Since the trams at Preston have been replaced by Leyland gearless buses, the corporation is now busily engaged in removing the tramlines. After their removal the lines are towed by a 1919 Leyland lorry to the breaking-up yard. Some of the lines have been sold to builders of housing estates and will be used as girders in the construction of buildings.' The photo is thought to date from around 1936, and the hand-written caption on the back reads: 'Articulated six-wheeler?' *Ian Allan Library*

Left:
Inside Bradford's Thornbury depot in October 1966, No 543 (EKU 543), an AEC Regent III/NCB double-decker cut down to become a pole-painters' lorry. To its left are trolleybuses 755 (FKU 755), a 1950 BUT 9611T/Weymann, and 801 (BDJ 89), an ex-St Helens 1951 BUT 9611T/East Lancs.
P. J. Thompson

Right:
This 1931 Thornycroft BC, originally with a Northern Counties single-deck body, was withdrawn from passenger service in 1945, becoming a pole carrier for Cardiff Corporationin 1946 and surviving until 1958 in this rôle. In the background is one of Cardiff's famous East Lancs-bodied BUT 9641T single-deck trolleybuses. *A. N. Porter*

Left:
Used by Bournemouth as a pole carrier, complete with mobile crane, Bournemouth Corporation FRU 224 was new in 1943. A Guy Arab, originally with Weymann double-deck body, it had ended its passenger days as an open-topper. *D. R. Harvey*

Above:
A rather more straightforward truck: a Ford D-series in the West Midlands PTE fleet. No 229 (HOA 97N), with on-board crane for loading heavy materials on to the platform, was used for construction and repair work. *Ian Allan Library*

Left:
A poling vehicle, used in the erection and maintenance of trolleybus traction poles, in the Wolverhampton Corporation fleet. New in 1934 as a single-deck bus, Daimler COG5/Park Royal No 193 (JW 5793) joined the service fleet in 1948 and lasted in this rôle until 1961. *Alan D. Broughall*

Mobile canteens

Although the use of mobile canteens was not widespread, in certain towns and cities, often as a result of geography, they were an essential and welcome sight for bus crews.

Municipalities with routes terminating in town and city centres often provided mobile canteens for their staff at significant points. Most of these canteens were mobile in terms of their ability to get to the required point; once there they were immobile, waiting for customers. Some never moved at all, and it is doubtful if they could, under their own steam.

Fitted with water tanks and connected up to mains electricity, they provided a welcome break for drivers and conductors. Today, concern for the environment would outlaw them — though fortunately the number of food outlets has increased to the point where facilities of this type are unnecessary.

Above:
An Austin 16 saloon car converted to become a mobile canteen for Nottingham City Transport during World War 2. The word 'Nottingham' is not included in the fleetname, presumably as a wartime security measure, but the vehicle is fully painted with transfers in the undertaking's distinctive sans-serif typeface.
Ian Allan Library

77

Left:

Photographed in Cannon Street, Manchester, in June 1949, this Crossley with rear-entrance Crossley bodywork was new to Manchester Corporation in 1929 as No 149 (VR 2627), and saw out its final days as employees' canteen No A86. Note the power supply fed in from the right. VR 2627 was notable as the first all-Crossley bus built, being a 1929 Crossley Six. It had been fitted out as the Transport Committee coach and was also used as an illuminated bus between 1933 and 1935, before being withdrawn in 1937 for use as a permanent illuminated bus. Used as an ARP instruction bus in 1939/40, it was reinstated as a bus in 1941, was out on loan in 1942, and in 1943 became a mobile canteen. It appears in its illuminated guise on page 93.
D. F. Tee

Below:

Another Manchester canteen bus — VR 5742 (No A87), a 1930 Leyland Tiger TS2 with Manchester Corporation-built body, seen at Chorlton Street bus station. Its survival in this form allowed it to be rescued for preservation, and it is now in the Manchester Museum of Transport collection. *Michael Dryhurst*

Above:

With various city-centre termini, Manchester Corporation needed several buses for canteen duties. No 782 (FVM 312), a 1939 Crossley Mancunian with MCCW/Crossley body, had become mobile canteen A89 by the time it was photographed in Piccadilly. *D. R. Harvey collection*

Below:

Used as a canteen bus by SHMD Board, Thornycroft CTU 931 is seen in Hyde in 1958. *G. Lumb collection*

Above:

SHMD Board FTU 132, a Northern Counties-bodied Daimler COG6, seen at Hyde bus station in 1964 as a canteen bus — though drivers and conductors may have been less than happy to be interrupted by the public making enquiries. *T. G. Turner*

Below:

Belfast Corporation No 145 (GZ 1012), a 1943 Bedford OWB with SMT-built utility body, was withdrawn in 1949 and became mobile canteen No MC50. It is seen here in Donegal Square South in 1951. Note what appears to be a water tank on the roof and steps at the rear, suggesting entry was through the emergency door in the rear wall. *Alan B. Cross*

Nottingham City Transport DAU 455 was an AEC Regal O662 new in 1937 with Cravens bodywork as bus No 76. Following its withdrawal in 1953, it served as mobile canteen No 812 between 1956 and 1968.
Roy Marshall

Below:
A former municipal bus in use as a canteen for another operator, in this case BET-owned North Western Road Car at Lower Moseley Street coach station in Manchester. Seen in August 1961, DDK 117 was an ex-Rochdale Corporation 1938 Leyland Titan TD5 with Eastern Coach Works body. *R. L. Wilson*

Vans

Rather like lorries in municipal bus fleets, the vans were usually bought off-the-shelf and were used as transport between, say, the head office and the workshops and garages, carrying mail and other papers.

Occasionally a bus might be converted into a van where a more substantial vehicle was required, perhaps for cash carrying.

Some municipalities ran their own parcels service, providing a door-to-door service using a network of local shops as agents.

Included in this section are minibuses (some non-PSV), again usually off-the-shelf vehicles used for crew transfers or for local councillors and officials.

Above:

Grimsby-Cleethorpes No 2 (XEE 378V), a Leyland Sherpa, at Victoria Street depot in October 1984. *G. B. Wise*

Below:

A later Grimsby-Cleethorpes van, Ford Transit FBE 307Y, No 1 in the fleet. *G. B. Wise*

Top left:

Wolverhampton Corporation 1721 JA was a Morris J2VM van bought in 1959. *S. N. J. White*

Left:

A similar vehicle, an Austin Omnicoach, 710 CPT, was used by Stockton Corporation for transporting bus crews to changeover points at the end of shifts and picking up bus crews in the morning and taking them home late at night. It was fitted with a Perkins 1.6-litre Four 99 diesel engine, and the corporation's general manager and engineer claimed that it did work equivalent to double the normal work of a delivery van. Fuel consumption was claimed to be approximately 37mpg.
Ian Allan Library

Right:
Several municipalities operated commercial parcel services. SELNEC PTE's sizeable Parcels operation at Parr's Wood is seen in 1978. *Ian Allan Library*

Below:
Darlington Transport D998 EAJ, a Ford Transit crew bus used for contract hire. *Roy Marshall*

Other departments

The old corporation set-up meant that different departments worked closely together, and there were many occasions on which the transport department, with its mechanical knowledge and well-equipped workshops, was called upon to provide vehicles and facilities for other departments. It was not unusual for, say, the corporation's private cars —

Below:
Used by Barrow-in-Furness Health Service as a mobile child-welfare centre, Leyland Tiger bus EO 5401 was converted by its former owner, Barrow Corporation.
Ian Allan Library

from the Lord Mayor's down — to be maintained and garaged by the transport undertaking. Other vehicles — from dustcarts to park-keepers' vans to school buses — might also come into the chief engineer's remit.

Thus, when another department needed a specialised big vehicle, it would turn to the transport department for a bus, and for a conversion. Mobile libraries were the most obvious uses for older buses; they needed a walk-in space, and the coachbuilders would relish the chance to turn their hands to something different. There were also examples of buses converted for use as mobile toilets for special events, and as health centres for the public health department.

Below:
Barrow also converted one of its Leyland-bodied Royal Tiger buses, EO 9766, for use by the corporation's library service.
Ian Allan Library

Top left:
Preston Corporation converted Leyland Lion bus CK 4649 into a Travelling Library.
G. Lumb collection

Below left:
This 1936 Wigan Corporation Leyland Tiger, JP 1213, was converted to a mobile library for Leigh Corporation. The conversion was carried out by Leigh's transport department.
Ian Allan Library

Bottom left:
This 1944 Great Yarmouth Guy Arab II/Strachans, EX 5264, was in use in 1968 as a mobile library in its home town. *Ian Allan Library*

Top and Bottom right:
Photographed in June 1962 at Millhouses, Sheffield City Libraries MWA 756, a 1950 Leyland Tiger PS2/Strachans from the Sheffield 'B' fleet.
K. W. Swallow

Odds and ends

These are the vehicles that could be found in some — but by no means all — municipal fleets.

Double-deckers were converted into open-toppers — as tree-loppers or as wagons for lubricating the overhead. Retired buses were kept in reserve and fitted with snowploughs, ready to go into action in the event of a significant snowfall. Permanent-way men and other groups of employees required to work out on the streets needed somewhere to keep their coats and somewhere to enjoy a cigarette and eat their lunch — so old buses were kept on as mobile (and sometimes not-so-mobile) huts.

Below:
Used as a lubrication wagon for the trolleybus overhead, Belfast Corporation No LW29 (CZ 36) was formerly bus No 69, a 1932 AEC Regent 661 with Park Royal body. It was used in this form between 1946 and 1953 and is seen in Royal Avenue. *W. J. Wyse*

Centre right:
Wolverhampton Corporation FJW 561, a Guy Arab III with Guy body, was new as bus No 561 in 1949, and on withdrawal in 1963 became a mobile canteen and snowplough. It was withdrawn in 1971. *R. F. Mack*

Snowfalls may have been a problem in West Bromwich in the 1950s. Three corporation buses in Oak Lane depot in 1954 fitted with snowploughs and presumably not over-used. The double-deckers are Nos 60, 59 (EA 7666/5), 1936 Daimler COG5s with MCCW bodies, both converted for this purpose on withdrawal from the passenger fleet in 1952; the single-decker was No 129 (JW 8114), a 1936 Daimler COG5/Park Royal acquired from Wolverhampton Corporation in 1944, and used as a snowplough from 1950. All three were withdrawn in 1958.
D. R. Harvey collection

Right:
Blackpool Corporation's DFV 146, one of 100 Leyland PD2/3 Titans bought in 1949/50 with centre-entrance Burlingham bodies, in use as permanent way vehicle No 6 on the North Shore, with the tramway visible on the left. Several generations of Blackpool double-decker have been used for this purpose — and still are today, providing shelter and transport for the tramway's permanent-way gang. *Alan B. Cross*

Above:
An unusual Walsall Corporation conversion — No 231, a 1951 Guy Arab III/Park Royal, seen in Birchills depot in use as a vacuum-cleaning plant. It was withdrawn in 1967. *Alan D. Broughall*

Below:
Tree-loppers were used by many corporations. Coventry No 01 (EKV 963), a 1944 Daimler CWA6 rebodied by Roe in 1951, became a tree-lopper when it was withdrawn from passenger service in 1958, lasting in this form until 1967. *C. D. Mann*

Decorated buses

Long before buses first appeared carrying overall paid-for advertising, municipalities regularly decorated trams, motorbuses and trolleybuses to mark significant events. The vehicles used might have been pensioned off, but were sometimes still in the active fleet.

Royal occasions were popular — Jubilees and Coronations, for instance.

Cup-winning football teams were celebrated and transported in suitably decorated buses. Local appeals — the Lord Mayor's Appeal, a mass X-ray drive, a National Savings promotion — would call for a decorated vehicle.

Then there were the buses used for self-promotion, fitted out with desks and cameras to sell season tickets to commuters in the suburbs and town centres. And there have been exhibition buses, used to promote the undertaking or even, in some cases, available to other organisations for commercial hire.

Below:

An illuminated bus prepared by Manchester Corporation to celebrate Manchester City's FA Cup Final win in 1934. The figure is apparently that of the City captain and was life-size. Underneath is No 149 (VR 2627), which, as mobile canteen No A86, appears on page 78. *Ian Allan Library*

Above:
Temporarily decorated to celebrate the Silver Jubilee of King George V and Queen Mary in 1935, Leicester No 68 (JF 5010), a 1933 Leyland Titan TD3 with MCCW body. *D. R. Harvey collection*

Below:
Sitting in Nottingham's Parliament Square in 1957 in the company of two recently-delivered AEC Regent Vs with Park Royal bodywork is DAU 454, a 1937 AEC Regal/Cravens decorated as a Diamond Jubilee float, celebrating the start of municipal tramway operation in 1897. *Roy Marshall*

Above:
Somewhere under the loyal decorations celebrating the Queen's Coronation in June 1953 is West Bromwich No 32 (EA 4181), a 1929 Dennis ES with Dixon body, which, the original caption tells us, had 1,400 bulbs operated off 12-volt batteries.
Ian Allan Library

Right:
No 32 survives in preservation, and is seen filling up on an early Trans-Pennine Run.
Gavin Booth

Above:
Already featured on page 92 as a tree-lopper, Coventry EKV 963, a 1944 Daimler CWA6 with 1951 Roe body, is seen as a carol bus at Christmas 1959, being given a send-off by the Lord Mayor.
T. W. Moore

Left:
Decorated to promote Leeds Savings Week in 1955, AEC Regent/Roe No 263 (GUA 788, on tradeplates 0749 U) at Bramley.
R. F. Mack

Above:
**Promoting a British Rail Saver
ticket of £9 from Stoke-on-Trent to
London Euston, Chester
Corporation No 1 (RFM 641),
a 1953 Guy Arab IV with Massey
body. This bus is now preserved.**
Ian Allan Library

Right:
**Although ex-Rawtenstall
Corporation No 45 (DTD 249),
a Leyland-bodied Tiger TS8c, had
been withdrawn in 1955, it was
apparently still in use as an office
when photographed in June 1971.**
M. A. Penn

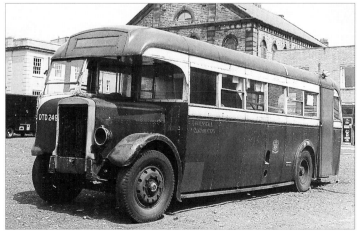

Left:
West Midlands PTE used this former Birmingham City Transport 1950 Guy Arab IV/MCCW, No 197 (JOJ 548), to publicise its one-week and four-week Travelcards. This bus is now preserved. *Ian Allan Library*

Below left:
Derby City Transport No 8179 (KRC 179D), a 1966 Daimler Fleetline/ Roe, fitted out as the Derby Photofare Bus, with equipment for photographing season-ticket holders. *D. J. Stanier*

Right:
Another West Midlands PTE Travelcard bus, ex-Birmingham JOJ 820, a 1952 Daimler CVG6/Crossley, allowed passengers to buy their tickets on board. No 196 is seen at Aldridge. *Adrian Pearson*

Below:
Leicester No 227 (MUT 227W), a brand-new Dennis Dominator/ East Lancs, toured the city's suburbs promoting the East Midlands Home Life exhibition before it entered service in 1980. *M. W. Greenwood*

Top left:
Pretending to be a Class 141 diesel multiple-unit alongside the real thing at a BREL Doncaster Works open day is 1976 West Yorkshire PTE No 47 (MUA 47P), a Bristol LHS6L/ECW. *M. W. Greenwood*

Top left:
Pretending to be a Class 141 diesel multiple-unit alongside the real thing at a BREL Doncaster Works open day is 1976 West Yorkshire PTE No 47 (MUA 47P), a Bristol LHS6L/ECW. *M. W. Greenwood*

Bottom left:
Ex-Lancashire United Bristol RESL6G/Plaxton No 248 (CTE 474E), converted by LUT into a mobile ticket and information office for Greater Manchester PTE, at Hindley in August 1980. *T. E. Sutch*

Above right:
Tyne & Wear PTE's mobile exhibition unit, named Exhibus, was 1972 Leyland National No E1819 (KBB 519L), seen here with its trailer/generator. *Ian Allan Library*

Below:
Greater Glasgow PTE No LA751 (NGB 119M), a new Leyland Atlantean AN68/1R with Alexander body, ready to leave for Glasgow Week in Hamburg in 1974. *Ian Allan Library*

Stretching a point

Merseyside PTE inherited ferry operations from the former Birkenhead and Wallasey corporations. Best known was probably the *Royal Iris*, seen here setting off from Liverpool's Pier Head. Note the MPTE logo on the funnel.
Ian Allan Library

The photographs in this section show some of the more dubious 'ancillary' vehicles that would not easily fit into any other category.

There is Merseyside PTE's *Royal Iris* ferry — and its rubber-tyred equivalent. There are taxi-cabs operated by local-authority fleets, and there are buses sent out to allow other operators to inspect them.

Below:

Wallasey Corporation 'disguised' Leyland Titan PD2/1 bus No 127 (AHF 365) as the *Royal Iris* and used it to tour Britain, promoting New Brighton as a holiday destination. *R. L. Wilson*

Below:

In the 1980s Lincoln City Transport operated its Limo services, linking the city centre with Hykeham and Brant Road. Here two FX4 taxicabs, D578/90 CRW, wait at the central bus station in 1986. *M. Fowler*

103

Above:
The second Carbodies taxi for Merseyside PTE's Merseylink service was YAC 349X. This style of taxi was a possible replacement for the FX4, and was produced in limited numbers for evaluation. *L. J. Long*

Below:
Southport Corporation's famous Ainsdale Beach service used Bedford QL buses built in 1946/7 with Rimmer, Harrison & Sutherland 23/24-seat bodies — not strictly ancillary vehicles, but hardly conventional PSVs. No 1 (EWM 680) is seen when new in 1946. *Ian Allan Library*

Top right:
Glasgow Corporation No TB35 (later registered FYS 765 and renumbered TBS1), a 1950 BUT RETB1 with Weymann two-door standee body, was demonstrated on the SLT trolleybus system at Atherton in March 1951, as seen here. *Ian Allan Library*

Bottom right:
Another Glasgow Corporation experimental vehicle, Daimler Freeline D650H No DS44 (FYS 521) with Alexander body, visits Dundee to demonstrate to officials and councillors.
Gavin Booth collection

Case History 1: Birmingham

The size of the Birmingham City Transport fleet reflected the size and importance of the city. Although it operated trolleybuses and built up a substantial tramway system, by the mid-1950s it was all-motorbus, with roundly 1,800 vehicles. Outside London, only a few bus fleets came anywhere near this total — Alexanders and Glasgow Corporation in Scotland, and, significantly, BMMO (Midland Red), also Birmingham-based.

With so many vehicles, Birmingham City Transport (BCT) required a substantial ancillary fleet. In addition to the predictable recovery vehicles, tower wagons and driving-tuition buses, there were vans of various sizes, including welding vans and bank vans, and lorries for a variety of purposes. Many of the ancillary vehicles were converted from motorbuses — indeed the BCT lives of many of the huge prewar Daimler COG5 fleet were prolonged when they were converted into different guises.

BCT formed the major part of the new West Midlands PTE when the latter was set up in 1969.

Above:

This ADC 507, OX 1536, was new in 1927 to Birmingham City Transport (BCT) as a double-deck bus with Buckingham body. Withdrawn from passenger service in 1935, it then became a welding van — No 17 in the service fleet — and performed these duties until 1947. It is seen at Digbeth in November 1939.
D. R. Harvey collection

Left:
Another former BCT bus, 1931 AEC Renown MV 489 (it was originally a demonstrator) seen in High Street in July 1953 on tradeplates 925 OP as a mobile crane, No 15. When new it had a Brush double-deck body.
J. C. Gillham

Below:
Seen in the late 1950s, BCT's No 14, an AEC Matador crane, on tradeplates 924 OP.
D. R. Harvey collection

Right:
Not, as it might seem, a bus in a scrapyard, but BCT's 'turn-over' bus, used to give recovery staff experience in righting overturned buses. It was new in 1934 as No 617 (AOG 617), one of a large fleet of Daimler COG5 buses with MCCW bodies. After withdrawal from passenger service it was used for vehicle recovery at Holford Drive, where it is seen in July 1954.
D. R. Harvey collection

Another of the same batch of Northern Counties-bodied COG5s, AOG 679, formerly bus No 679, was new in 1935 and withdrawn in 1946 for conversion to a bank van, service vehicle No 83. It was used in this way until 1967, when it was acquired for preservation. It is seen at the General Post Office in Victoria Square late in its BCT life. *Alan D. Broughall*

A later BCT COG5, 1937 MCCW-bodied No 988 (COX 988) became a snowplough after it was withdrawn from passenger service in 1954, surviving until 1963. *L. Mason*

Above:

Underneath this 1937 Coronation float is yet another BCT COG5, CVP 118 (No 1018), a 1937 example — presumably before it received its MCCW body. *D. R. Harvey collection*

Below:

BCT No 1383 (FOP 383), a Guy Arab II with Brush utility body, in use as a driver-training bus in October 1953. *B. W. Ware*

Edinburgh Corporation Transport Department (ECT) operated trams (until 1956) and buses between 1919 and 1975, when local government reorganisation created Lothian Region Transport. The importance of the tramways in the years before the 1950s meant that most ancillary vehicles were tram-related — tower wagons, lorries and tippers — and, of course, there were works trams: a water car, a welding car, two grinder cars and a salt car.

When the bus fleet grew in importance, more breakdown wagons were added to the fleet, and the driver-training fleet grew. For many years ECT provided Traffic Patrol vans for inspectors; at various times these were Trojans, Hillman Huskies and Land Rovers.

Above:
Used by Edinburgh Corporation Transport (ECT) as a bothy — a workmen's hut — is this 1929 AEC Reliance 660 with Croall body. These bothies were towed to the site of the work, in this case Frederick Street, replacing cobbles after lifting tramlines in April 1953. *J. C. Gillham*

Left:
Used in the 1950s by the city's Lighting & Cleansing Department as a mobile toilet during Edinburgh Festival, for visitors to the Military Tattoo, ex-ECT No G23 (WS 6383), a 1935 Daimler COG6/MCCW. The external staircase suggests that some of its customers — possibly the ladies — used the upper deck. *Gavin Booth*

Above:

Not strictly a municipal ancillary vehicle, but a magnificent specimen nonetheless. CVA 801 was the former War Department Albion CX24 tank transporter used with a specially-constructed trailer by James N. Connell to collect Edinburgh's trams at the western extremity of the tramway, at the Maybury, to transport them to Coatbridge for scrapping. Once driven into the trailer, the tram was jacked up clear of the roadway. *Gavin Booth collection*

Left:

The ECT 'learner' fleet in the late 1950s — 1945 Guy Arab II ESC 132 (formerly No 83) with Northern Counties body, and 1941 Bristol L5G DSF 987 (No 861) with Bristol body. The Bristol was withdrawn in 1961 but the Guy survived until 1967. *Gavin Booth*

Above:

The black-painted Perkins-engined Trojan vans used by ECT for traffic-patrol work were familiar throughout the city. LWS 382 is seen in the 1950s at Edinburgh Zoo on a busy summer's day, assisting with the loading of MCW Orion-bodied Leyland Titan PD2/20 No 438 (LFS 438)
Gavin Booth collection

Right:

ECT had two of these Trojan 25cwt minibuses, bought new in 1961. Never used in public service, they were used for transporting councillors and officials, as part of the ECT-administered City Car fleet. WSC 914 stands at Marine garage in 1963. *Gavin Booth*

Left:
This Land Rover was used in ECT's Traffic Patrol fleet in the 1960s and 1970s. New in 1966, GSG 477D, seen here at The Mound being passed by ECT's prototype Leyland Atlantean/ Alexander, No 801, was also used to tow vehicles. *Gavin Booth*

Inset and below:
Two of ECT's 1948 Guy Arab III/ MCCWs were used as training vehicles between 1961 and 1970. No 839 (ESG 652) is seen in George Street. The interior view shows the cut-away bulkhead behind the driver's cab, with the gear positions chalked on the bulkhead. This bus is now in preservation. *Gavin Booth*

Above and below:

Five of the 1948 MCCW-bodied Guy Arab III single-deckers were converted into road gritters. No 2 (ESG 646, formerly bus No 833) is seen at Marine garage with its gritter body and glassfibre Leyland-style front. *Gavin Booth*

Above:
A later generation of Edinburgh trainer, TB3 (JSC 853E, formerly bus No 853), a 1967 Leyland Atlantean PDR1/1 with Alexander body, seen in 1983 in use with Lothian Region Transport, pulling on to Princes Street from Leith Street. Behind it is 1957 Leyland Titan PD2/20 with MCCW body, OFS 795, in use with the region's Social Work Department as a Playbus. *Ian Train*

Right:
Running on tradeplates 153 S, Lothian's Leyland Super Comet tow truck hauls 1966 Leyland Atlantean PDR1/1 No 818 (EWS 818D) up towards Leith Street in March 1980.
A. J. Douglas

Huddersfield Corporation operated trams, motorbuses and trolleybuses, though technically it was the Huddersfield Joint Omnibus Committee (JOC), formed in 1929 by the corporation and the LMS railway, that operated the motorbuses. In 1940 the trams were finally replaced by trolleybuses, and in 1968 the last trolleybuses were replaced by motorbuses. In that same year the JOC was discontinued when the corporation took over the state-owned interests.

In 1974 Huddersfield Corporation was merged with other municipal undertakings to form West Yorkshire PTE.

The Huddersfield ancillary fleet is well-documented, and included tower wagons, lorries and recovery vehicles, and vans — not to mention six pedal cycles that were used to guide convoys of trolleybuses on the Bradley route in thick fog!

Many of the tower wagons — typically AECs, in the later years — were bought new, although some were converted motorbuses.

Lorries included a Morris used for refuelling motorbuses at town termini, and others used as gritters and for general purposes.

Vans were usually bought new for the various departments in the transport undertaking — overhead, traffic, stores, inspectors.

Below:
Huddersfield tower wagon No 2 (CX 3118) was a locally-built Karrier WDS, new in 1919 and withdrawn by 1932. *G. Lumb collection*

This 1925 Morris 1-ton lorry (CX 7638) was initially used by Huddersfield to deliver petrol from its 200-gallon tank, in the days when petrol-engined buses had to be refuelled in service. Not surprisingly, perhaps, this practice was banned after a number of fires, and from 1930 the vehicle was used as a lorry. This official view (*below***) shows without its registration number and carrying its original tank; this proved to be too small, so the larger tank seen in the rear-end photo was fitted.**
G. Lumb collection

Above:
The working end of tower wagon No 3 (CX 5527), a 1923 Karrier H. *G. Lumb collection*

Right:
Bought new in 1938, tower wagon No 5 (BCX 113) was an AEC Monarch with an Eagle body and tower.
G. Lumb collection

DANGER
OVERHEAD
REPAIRS

DANGER OVERHEAD REPAIRS

Left and below:
Official photos of Huddersfield No 10 (MVH 387), a 1958 AEC Mandator with Eagle body and tower. *G. Lumb collection*

Right:
Huddersfield Corporation's 1958 AEC Mandator tower wagon No 9 (MVH 388) tows a trolleybus. *J. Saunders*

Below right:
A formal portrait of Huddersfield recovery wagon No A10 (actually MVH 387, but normally used, as here, on tradeplates 153 VH). A 1958 AEC Mandator, it started life as a tower wagon — see the previous pictures — and was converted into a recovery vehicle in 1964. *G. Lumb collection*

Above:
**Huddersfield Corporation AEC tow truck No A8
(on tradeplates 373 VH), with a damaged Seddon RU
on suspended tow and tower wagon A9 following,
in June 1973.** *G. Lumb collection*

Below:
**This 1962 Austin 15cwt Omnivan, No A3 (XCX 435),
was in the Huddersfield ancillary fleet from 1962,
when it was bought new, to 1971.** *G. Lumb collection*

Appendix - The municipal bus operators

The 98 municipal bus operators listed below represent the maximum number in the post-World War 2 years. The municipal list stayed fairly steady for a number of years, with only a few local boundary re-shuffles. Grimsby merged with Cleethorpes in 1957, Hartlepool with West Hartlepool in 1967, and Haslingden with Rawtenstall to become Rossendale in 1968. West Bridgford was taken over by Nottingham in 1968, and Middlesbrough, Stockton and the Tees-side Railless Traction Board were combined as Teesside Municipal Transport in 1968; the latter would be renamed Cleveland Transit in 1974. Further local reorganisation brought the Halifax and Calderdale undertakings together as Calderdale in 1971.

In 1970, meanwhile, the newly-formed National Bus Company had acquired two municipalities — Exeter and Luton.

In 1969/70 the first four Passenger Transport Executives (PTEs) had been set up, absorbing 20 municipal fleets. These were Merseyside PTE, SELNEC (South East Lancashire, North East Cheshire) PTE, Tyneside PTE and West Midlands PTE.

The next new PTE was Greater Glasgow, set up in 1973. Two more English PTEs were created in 1974, absorbing a further eight undertakings, and existing PTE areas were enlarged to include other municipalities. The new PTEs were South Yorkshire PTE and West Yorkshire PTE. Merseyside PTE gained St Helens and Southport, Wigan passed to Greater Manchester PTE (formerly SELNEC), Sunderland was absorbed by Tyne & Wear PTE (formerly Tyneside) and Coventry disappeared into West Midlands PTE.

Major government reorganisation altered council boundaries and names in England and Wales in 1974. Few municipal bus companies continued to operate under their former names, and others found themselves brought together under new, enlarged councils.

A similar exercise in Scotland in 1975 resulted in Regions assuming control for transport in Aberdeen, Dundee and Edinburgh.

The situation remained fairly stable until the time of deregulation in 1986, when arm's-length municipal companies were set up in the remaining operations. For some this was a prelude to privatisation — sometimes involving management and employees, sometimes involving a third party. Many of the former local-authority operations have now been absorbed by the major groups. Arriva has Colchester, Derby, Merseyside and Southend; Blazefield has Burnley & Pendle and Hyndburn; FirstGroup has Aberdeen, Glasgow, Great Yarmouth, Greater Manchester (part), Leicester, Northampton, Portsmouth, South Yorkshire, Southampton and West Yorkshire; Go-Ahead has Brighton; National Express has Dundee and West Midlands; Stagecoach has Barrow, Chesterfield, Cleveland Transit, Greater Manchester (part), Grimsby-Cleethorpes, Hartlepool, Kingston-upon-Hull, Lancaster and Tyne & Wear; Yorkshire Traction has Lincoln. Some continue as separately-branded entities while others have been absorbed into local groupings.

In Northern Ireland, the Belfast Corporation undertaking became Citybus in 1973, as part of the Northern Ireland Transport Holding Co. One other bus-operating municipality in the British Isles was Douglas Corporation, which still operates the famous Douglas horse tramway but passed its bus operations to Isle of Man National Transport in 1976.

Those municipal operators prefixed with an * in the listing below are still in local-authority ownership; many of the others can still be traced to parts of bigger companies, while a few simply gave up the unequal struggle and ceased trading altogether. Operators marked + once ran trolleybuses.

The first column in the list shows the name used in the 1950s, and the second column shows name changes while still under local-authority control.

Aberdare+	Cynon Valley 1974
Aberdeen	Grampian 1975
Accrington	Hyndburn 1974
Ashton-under-Lyne+	SELNEC PTE 1969
Barrow	
Bedwas & Machen	Rhymney Valley 1974
Belfast+	
Birkenhead	Merseyside PTE 1969
Birmingham+	West Midlands PTE 1969
*Blackburn	
*Blackpool	
Bolton	SELNEC PTE 1969
*Bournemouth+	
Bradford+	West Yorkshire PTE 1974
Brighton+	
Burnley, Colne & Nelson	Burnley & Pendle 1974
Burton upon Trent	East Staffordshire 1974
Bury	SELNEC PTE 1969
Caerphilly	Rhymney Valley 1974
*Cardiff+	
*Chester	
Chesterfield+	
Cleethorpes+	Grimsby-Cleethorpes 1957
Colchester	
Colwyn Bay	

Coventry	West Midlands PTE 1974
Darlington+	
Darwen	Blackburn 1974
Derby+	
Doncaster+	South Yorkshire PTE 1974
Douglas	
Dundee+	Tayside
*Eastbourne	
Edinburgh	*Lothian
Exeter	
Gelligaer	Rhymney Valley 1974
Glasgow+	Greater Glasgow PTE 1973
Great Yarmouth	
Grimsby+	Grimsby-Cleethorpes 1957
Halifax+	West Yorkshire PTE 1974
Hartlepool+ (Borough)	Hartlepool (County Borough) 1967
Haslingden	Rossendale 1968
Huddersfield+	West Yorkshire PTE 1974
*Ipswich+	
Kingston-upon-Hull+	
Lancaster	
Leeds+	West Yorkshire PTE 1974
Leicester	
Leigh	SELNEC PTE 1969
Lincoln	
Liverpool	Merseyside PTE 1969
Llandudno	Aberconwy 1974
Lowestoft	Waveney 1974
Luton	
Lytham St Annes	Fylde 1974
Maidstone+	
Manchester+	SELNEC PTE 1969
Merthyr Tydfil	
Middlesbrough	Teesside 1968
Morecambe & Heysham	Lancaster 1974
Newcastle upon Tyne+	Tyneside PTE 1970
*Newport	

Northampton	
*Nottingham+	
Oldham	SELNEC PTE 1969
*Plymouth	
Pontypridd+	Taff Ely 1974
Portsmouth+	
Preston	
Ramsbottom+	SELNEC PTE 1969
Rawtenstall	*Rossendale 1968
*Reading+	
Rochdale	SELNEC PTE 1969
Rotherham+	South Yorkshire PTE 1974
St Helens+	Merseyside PTE 1974
Salford	SELNEC PTE 1969
Sheffield	South Yorkshire PTE 1974
South Shields+	Tyneside PTE 1970
Southampton	
Southend+	
Southport	Merseyside PTE 1974
SHMD	SELNEC PTE 1969
Stockport+	SELNEC PTE 1969
Stockton-on-Tees	Teesside 1968
Sunderland	Tyneside PTE 1973
Swindon	*Thamesdown 1974
Tees-side RTB+	Teesside 1968
Todmorden	West Yorkshire PTE 1974
Wallasey	Merseyside PTE 1969
Walsall+	West Midlands PTE 1969
*Warrington	Warrington
West Bridgford	Nottingham 1968
West Bromwich	West Midlands PTE 1969
West Hartlepool	Hartlepool (County Borough) 1967
West Monmouthshire	*Islwyn 1974
Widnes	*Halton 1974
Wigan+	Greater Manchester PTE 1974
Wolverhampton+	West Midlands PTE 1969